Gravity/Levity

poems by

Anne Bakeman

Finishing Line Press
Georgetown, Kentucky

Gravity/Levity

*for Paul,
and in memory of my sister Dot*

"What matters in life is not what happens to you
but what you remember and how you remember it."
—Gabriel García Márquez

"Sometimes when I'm sad, the dead leaves
in the bed of my pickup get up on their own
and start dancing."
—Ted Kooser, from his poem "A Dervish of Leaves"

Copyright © 2022 by Anne Bakeman
ISBN 979-8-88838-055-0 First Edition
All rights reserved under International and Pan-American Copyright Conventions. No part of this book may be reproduced in any manner whatsoever without written permission from the publisher, except in the case of brief quotations embodied in critical articles and reviews.

ACKNOWLEDGMENTS

The poem "Rockaway" was previously published in the journal *Peregrine*.

Thanks to Julie Cadwallader Staub for getting me started on this path, and to my once-a-month poetry group and other friends, and of course my family, for keeping me going.

Publisher: Leah Huete de Maines
Editor: Christen Kincaid
Cover Art: Betsy Kane
Author Photo: Paul Bakeman
Cover Design: Elizabeth Maines McCleavy

Order online: www.finishinglinepress.com
also available on amazon.com

Author inquiries and mail orders:
Finishing Line Press
PO Box 1626
Georgetown, Kentucky 40324
USA

This chapbook was made possible in part by donations to the ONE LAST WORD Program. ONE LAST WORD helps to bring the last works of gifted poets to the world.

Table of Contents

Gravity/Levity	1
Rockaway	2
Girl at a Washtub	3
Old Year, New Year	4
house on lake road south	5
Johnny Mathis	6
Jitterbug Lessons	8
Together We Try to Round the Sharp Corners in Our Marriage*	10
When One Has Lived a Long Time with Others	11
Hermit Thrush	12
What Saves Us	13
Asters	14
Hawk Plucks Bird	15
Poison Ivy	16
Seiji Ozawa	17
Weather Lessons	19
The Under-Ten Soccer Girls	20
Speech	22
The Labyrinth at All Saints	23
One Thing Always Is More Important than Another	24
How a Poem Happens	25
May 11, 1987	26
too many poems about death	27
In the Medical Building	28
Sweeping the Sidewalk	29
To My Cancer	31
Infusion Room	32
ode to my bald head	33
Knotweed	34
Kindness	35
Washing Hands during the Pandemic	36
Daughter, Spinning	38
Women of a Certain Age	39
if you're not in the habit of saying I love you	40

Gravity/Levity

On a gray day, how easy it is to be
pulled down by the gravity of
your own despair, how
satisfying to wallow
in it, your swollen
face, your red
eyes acces-
sories to
your
mis-
ery

but
wait!
just now a
swath of blue
in the west lets
the sun burst forth
from above the clouds
scattering reflections and
brightness everywhere and
there's an aroma of hot cocoa
wafting from the kitchen and you
realize this is better and you want to
let out a guffaw but you don't because
it would be unseemly so soon following all
the keening and moaning, the gnashing of teeth.

Rockaway

In July my mother forgets how to swim.
She stands waist-deep and frail
in the lake's roped-off swimming area
which last summer she crossed
and re-crossed in tireless even strokes
and tells me with a strained laugh
that she can't seem to do it, as if she were

still the child she was at Rockaway
in the summer of '25 before she learned
how to move through water by parting it
with her arms, flutter-kicking her legs,
from the girl whose family had
a water-house on stilts. She says her feet
don't want to leave the ground.

I only have to get her started, because
no one unlearns how to swim,
but when I stop holding her, sandwich-like,
one hand on top and one beneath,
her chin goes under, and under again.
"Enough!" she sputters, flailing
upright. Hisses "Go!" and I'm gone,

thinking how can this be happening,
she was a good swimmer,
thinking maybe it won't come back to her,
thinking swim while you can, girl,
thinking I wish I could have been there
to see them in their old-fashioned
bathing costumes, caps like rubber helmets,

paddling the swells, shrieks drowned
in roaring surf. How they could swim
at all, saltwater incessantly rushing in,
swirling, crashing, pounding against them,
pounding the stilt-like pilings holding up
optimistically perched houses,
then rushing out again.

Girl at a Washtub
    —after a snapshot labeled "E. doing her wash, October, 1924"
    —for Nels, Diane and Terry

Caught in sepia memory at seven,
she poses behind a child-size washtub
perched on an upright wooden crate,

hands plunged in the by-now-tepid water,
intent on her work and squinting a bit
in the slant light of Indian Summer,

the wicker baby carriage parked nearby
nestling her doll, asleep and oblivious
on a plump pillow. Looming behind them,

fences—chain link, stockade—bisect
the backyards of the Moffat Street
tenements, some of the windows

adorned with shutters, others hooded
with awnings in sedate stripes
casting long shadows against the building.

The day is winding down.
Now the wind is picking up,
setting into billowing incandescence

the inverted white wall of laundry
suspended overhead across the yards
from a neighbor's upstairs window.

Shortly the girl will finish her chore,
gather up her doll and go inside.
Someone will reel in the fluttering clothes

and the scene will fade back to gray-
brown, until, perhaps, a girl appears
again, wash is hung out to dry,

there's a bit of wind.

Old Year, New Year

Where there was nothing last year,
suddenly there's this old paper, handwritten,
folded and stuffed in a dusty portfolio
and nearly tossed by me in a downsizing frenzy.
It's 1945, the war over, the children at the table
young, baby in the high chair, my mother 31
and pregnant, her faded script recording
a one-act play starring the ringing doorbell
and a mysterious man seen only by her:

Doorbell rings.
Middle child: "Who's that?"
Baby: "Dat!"
Mother goes to door, converses with man at door, returns to kitchen.
Oldest child: "Who was that?"
Baby: "Dat!"
Mother: "That was a man taking the dog census. He asked if we have a dog."
Oldest child: "We don't have a dog."
Middle child: "Yes we do."
Oldest child: "We do not."
Middle child (pointing to stuffed dog): "Yes we do!"
Oldest child (scornfully): "That's not a real dog!"
Baby (clapping): "Doggie!"

It goes on like that, the two older children
bickering, the baby chiming in, my mother
keeping the peace. Mere scrap of the past, I
never would have missed it if I hadn't come
across it, little piece of silliness, and yet how it
swirls me into that simpler world, how it
beams me onto the scuffed kitchen linoleum,
so tangible it feels, so real, only because
my mother bothered to write it down.

house on lake road south

it was a time of brownies and fairies
we found the signs in the hideout formed
by lilacs grown together next to the pasture
where cows with names like Daisy and Myrtle
did their contented grazing

we built twig houses for the tree spirits
beneath the horse chestnut whose giant limbs
almost touched the ground gathered us in
we filled our pockets with its shiny brown nuts
as if they were gold

took turns riding the hard-tire two-wheeler
chain-driven three-wheeler with a kid on the back
up and down the hollyhock-lined driveway
to far places across ocean prairie mountain sky
and what we didn't have we invented but not

the real Hoosier cabinet with built-in flour sifter
in the kitchen where our grandmother cooked up
her magic: no apples in the house one day
still she was mixing the dough as we left for school
But Grandma we said not true believers

and home we came to the aroma of *apfelkuchen*
wafting from the house filling the crisp air
for no sooner had she said *now I need apples*
when a truck came rollicking down the hill
hit a bump and just like that there were apples

the heifers lift their heads in mild surprise
the empty bushel somersaults into the pasture
the grandmother does a little dance in her sturdy black shoes
the apples bounce and roll across the grass toward the house
she crimps her apron and stoops to pick them all up

and then we grew up and went away and when we came
back they were gone: lilacs pasture house tree cows
in their place acres of parking lot gigantic store
we might have imagined them if we didn't remember
but we will remember

Johnny Mathis

at fifteen we wanted real work real money wanted
Everly Brothers Pat Boone Johnny Mathis 45s wanted
to own their smooth voices to play them over and over
the soundtrack to our dreams we were too young to count

pills for the pharmacist at Dobson's Rexall run the cash
register at Houston's 5 & 10 serve Cherry Cokes at
Bob's Soda Shop too money-mad to volunteer at the
migrant daycare in the Methodist Church basement

lining up small children we couldn't understand who
didn't cry didn't complain ate what was put in front
of them we filled out our working papers applied for farm
work picking sour cherries at Ganzinger's Orchards

we were working we had ladders we were assigned to trees
in a separate part of the orchard from the migrant workers
up North for the summer the only other people of color
we'd ever come across besides Edie and Clarice Mathis

who showed up at BHS every April disappeared in October
when asked said yes they were Johnny's cousins no they
never saw him anymore couldn't get his autograph for us
they said this in English we could understand when

we arrived in the morning the workers had been there
for hours we were half an orchard away they picked
circles around us we sneaked peeks they filled many
baskets to our one their covered arms their quick hands

a blur we fooled around loitered in the shade lingered
over our brown bag lunches wiped off the spray and
ate the imperfect fruit stayed only until three all we
were allowed it was enough when our mother came

to fetch us we were ready all night we picked cherries felt
their plump roundness in our hands smelled their
sour ripeness in our dreams by noon of the third day
we were finished the trees bare of cherries our hundred

dollar dreams crushed Mr. G paid us in cash said we
could hitch a ride into town on the back of the truck
heading to the canning factory the girl in the middle
gripping the floor for dear life the other two clutching

the side walls legs dangling three feet above ground
the truck lurching at the stoplight nearly tossing us off
down the Main Street hill into town angling right on two
wheels onto Park Avenue onto High Street where we could

stop screaming jump off smell the cannery in back billowing
pungent steam for days our fingers cramped from picking
from holding on from doing real work from fisting a few
dollars from grasping why people do this day in day out

Jitterbug Lessons
  —with thanks to instructor T.B.

1. Basic Step

At first, four steps to three beats is hard. They
can't make it work. She holds her arms too slack,
he keeps his stiff and tends to yank her back
too soon whenever she quick-steps away
from him. He sets his feet down hard, afraid
that if he doesn't, she might try to lead.
She likes to rock and jazz things up a tad
on the slow steps. He likes to play it straight.

2. Inside Swing

They love the way this feels: turning toward each other without turning
into each other. Stepping away quickly. Pulling back. Touching only hands.

3. Pass By

They start out well enough, face to face,
right hands joined, pulling each other behind
on the first slow step, minding
their moves. Turning away out of her space
and out of sight of him, she falls for the smooth
dancer to her left and doesn't come around
in time to catch his hand. When she's unwound,
they start again, trying to reclaim the mood.

4. Pretzel

Hands joined with his, she turns under
the first arch, is halfway through the second
when the woman in blue turns his head. She knows
the routine: stop in place, watch his back and wait
for him to turn himself around under their arch
of arms. Facing her again, he inside swings her
so fast she is dizzy and has to stop for breath.

5. Arm Slide

Standing right sides together, arms poised,
makes them feel equal. When she brings
her right arm down behind his head, she thinks
he looks a little taller than he used
to be. He thinks she looks pretty nice. Next
their hands slide down each other's arms and catch
and they balance in a quick-stepping match
of feet, noticing how their arms are flexed.

Together We Try to Round the Sharp Corners in Our Marriage
    —quote by Galina Gelfer, Russian emigree, in the Burlington Free Press

Upstairs the bathroom sits unfinished, a room
without a bath. I've been here before. Now

I raise the issue of its condition, reminding you
of what you said eons ago about wanting

to do it yourself, a project, something to
accomplish with your own hands. "These things

take time," you say again and the shower stalled
forever in a large box on my side of the bedroom

dissolves into the fiction whose intrinsic monetary
possibilities you think so highly of, wondering

why I do not try my hand at that instead of poetry
which puts food in the mouth of no one. "Poets

are the guardians of Truth," I say, as I've said before,
looking up from the story I am having trouble starting.

You slide a half-smile my way as you sidle past,
tilting ten feet of copper pipe to clear the stairwell.

When One Has Lived a Long Time with Others
—*after Galway Kinnell's poem "When One Has Lived a Long Time Alone"*

When one has lived a long time with others,
she is loathe to refrain from swatting the fly, or
she might prefer to scoop it into the spider web
that has become part of the scenery, just to see
what will happen: the resident spider rushing
from its corner to claim its windfall, the fly's
futile struggle to escape before paralysis sets in.
Nor should the virtues be expected to fare well:
Patience can be seen rolling her eyes at memory
lapses and the cap left off the toothpaste tube.
Sure, one rescues the toad and wraps in a towel
the swift that has fallen down the chimney
to gently set her flying free, but Forgiveness
may not extend a gracious hand to the one who
left the damper open. As for Gratitude: She must
work hard to pay attention to the small things—
a hundred bees humming in the Russian sage,
the perfect tomato ripening on the windowsill,
someone washing dishes without being asked—
when one has lived a long time with others.

Hermit Thrush
    —for Emilie

to hear it
you must enter
the cathedral hidden
deep in summer woods
at dusk

flute-like
mournful
haunting
these are only words

you will know it when
something like homesickness
stirs in you

oh holy holy
you long for your mother
you long for all the others
you have loved

ah purity purity
you long for your childhood
the childhood of your children

eeh sweetly sweetly
you long to lie down
in the soft moss
to remember
to listen

What Saves Us

Who knows if we will act in time
to stanch the rise of warming seas,
heal the exhausted air. The earth
is waiting, the time is short—and yet

just now in the midst of the forest
a lone hermit thrush sings its tiny heart out,
its otherworldly cadences growing louder
as I approach, piercing the solitude
until this is all that I can hear,

my own heart singing at the sound of it,
and I can't help myself: nothing matters
beyond this particular place, this songster,
this song.

Asters

It takes
a double-take
for you to believe
that they are glowing
the way that they are
their impossible purples
when you lean in closer
so gloriously luminous
in this autumnal light
that you wouldn't mind
lying down among them

not to miss the monarch
sailing in for a landing
folding and unfolding
its translucent wings
lingering a moment
before zigzagging
to the next one
before floating
into the wind
that hustles it
on its way

Hawk Plucks Bird
—Left Field Press Exclusive

Dateline South Burlington, April 30: A local woman's bird feeder was visited yesterday by what appeared to be a Cooper's hawk. The 15-inch accipiter glided into her Ridgewood yard, snatching a goldfinch from the feeder. "I was taking a break from writing poetry and got up to stretch my legs," the woman said. "I happened to glance out the window at just the right moment—five seconds earlier or later and I would have missed it." She said at first she thought the hawk was the shadow of a cloud moving overhead and only realized what had happened when it veered sharply upward to miss the garage; it was then that she saw the tiny bright yellow bird dangling from its talons. "There was not so much as a wingbeat until it rose over the parking lot," she said, reporting that she was "over-come with emotion" at the sight, first by anger at the hawk for having trespassed through her property, then by great sadness for the goldfinch, in his prime and with a family to feed, followed by guilt at providing a space to gather that small birds would assume to be safe. "It took a while," she said, "for the voyeur in me to be awakened by the marvelous serendipity of witnessing something so terrible and elegant." Quoting the poet Eamon Grennan*, she said, "Finally, 'that indifferent / singleminded glide of the hawk, / his one hunger' gave me to understand that this was simply the way of things, and I was able to turn my attention to the chicken parts thawing on the counter."

*from his poem "One Morning during the Elections"

Poison Ivy
>—*for Eric*

This time it was high winter in Ohio
when you caught it, burying the dog
above the horseshoe turn the river makes
around your adopted town. I wondered
how the ground could be broken; you said
you bought a shovel, dug a hole, slid
the body in, covered it, backfilled.

He wouldn't lie down that last night,
you said, so you took him for walks
in the slow dark to keep him
from going off to die alone.
In the morning you called the vet.
When his legs buckled, you cradled
his head. When it was over,
you carried him to the car.

According to the family joke,
you only had to look at it and hives
would appear. This time you must
have brushed against the big oak,
not noticing the vines the size of
forearms etching its trunk, or maybe
you cut through the roots as you dug.
Whatever it was, it was enough:
for days your body wept.

I would have been there for you,
but you told me long distance that
you had to get through this alone,
your voice so loud and clear
across the lines between us
you might have been next door.

Seiji Ozawa
    —for Jen

<u>*My story:*</u>

When you were five we took you to the festival at Tanglewood. We had lawn tickets because we didn't know how you'd be if we were seated in the Music Shed. You, the child who ran everywhere from the time you could walk, refused to sit on the blanket. Instead you lunged to the rope separating the Shed from the lawn and stood next to your brother as we had never seen you, straight and still as a tree, for the whole 45 minutes of Beethoven's Violin Concerto. Afterward, the Seiji Ozawa poster you clamored for hung on your wall for years; even in tatters you wouldn't let it be taken down.

<u>Your story:</u>

I was always fighting with my body
to slow down and hold still.
Here in this place it did not want to move.
The small man with his back to me
whose name was Seiji Ozawa
had flying black hair and
was always moving, like me,
but staying in one place
on his box called a podium.
Swaying, bending, jumping,
dancing with the man playing the violin,
waving his stick called a baton.
The music went into his baton
and came out right into me. Seiji Ozawa
was the music. He and the music
were the same thing.

I had to have the picture called a poster.
In the poster Seiji Ozawa was still
but he looked as if he was moving.
I stood next to the poster and cried
until they bought it for me.

I could hear the music when I looked
at the Seiji Ozawa poster. I could see him
moving while staying in one place.
I had to keep the poster even after
it was falling apart. If they took it away,
I knew the music would be gone.

Weather Lessons
> *"When you step out on the Earth, every step you take should be a prayer."*
> —Black Elk, Oglala Lakota spiritual leader
> *"When there's a storm, you should hold somebody's hand."*
> —Phoebe, age 3

1) Walk lightly, love, upon the sacred land.
Every step you take should be a prayer.
When there's a storm, hold onto someone's hand.

2) When vapor condenses, the spawned clouds may stand
forty thousand feet in the troposphere,
while lightning walks across the sacred land.

3) The Global Hawk weather drone (unmanned)
gathers data where conditions are severe.
If you are there, hold onto someone's hand!

4) Charge change between ionosphere and ground
drives a steady current, when weather's fair,
from atmosphere lightly down to sacred land.

5) When there's a storm, the charged Earth may send
charge upward in blue St. Elmo's Fire.
If you should see this, hold somebody's hand.

6) New clouds may tower, not ready yet to spend
their energy with the usual cloud-to-ground flair:
Walk lightly, love, upon the sacred land.
When there's a storm, hold onto someone's hand.

The Under-Ten Soccer Girls
   —for Phoebe

They come in different sizes
and run as if they mean it,
fast and hard or at an easy lope,
and when they catch up with the ball

they know what they have to do:
control it, pass it, move it toward
the other team's goal and away
from their own. Be fierce, be fair.

When the ball comes at them
they confront and deflect more,
flinch and recoil less, than they did
a few weeks ago. When the ball

goes out-of-bounds they call out
the name of the teammate
who will throw it back into play,
raising an arm to show they're

free, looking self-conscious and
serious, as if they've figured out
what they're doing and what
bigger thing they're a part of.

Sometimes they win, sometimes
they don't. At the end, win or lose,
they sing a loud cheer for their
opponents, joining hands to form

a bridge for the other team to
duck through, ducking through
the other team's bridge. They carry
out this ritual with enthusiastic grace.

The member of the team I know best
is running downfield now, all legs
in her baggy shorts and lucky
knee-highs. She loves this game,

this sport of skill and teamwork
and rules she's learned and abides by,
rules of the game and of acceptance,
growing up and fair play.

The world could learn something.

Speech
    —*for Eliza*

From her two-year-old mouth spill
big words we didn't know she knew.
Next to come are complete sentences.
"Why?" she asks, and if not satisfied
with our reply, "Why?" again, and
the wheels go around in her little head
while she thinks about it all. Then
the words again, flowing like honey.

Child-wizard, she keeps us mostly
agape, tongue-tied, on our toes.

Years have flown. She's growing up
and the words keep getting bigger,
the sentences longer. We listen, rapt,
for new and surprising utterances,
still as flabbergasted as ever,
trying our best not to miss anything.

She makes us wonder how it is
that speech comes so easily to one
child while another is unable to talk.
Reminds us to wish for all children—
those who speak and those who don't—
a way to be heard, to let us know,
to amaze us with what's inside.

The Labyrinth at All Saints

It must be years since we last walked it. Now
the bricks lining the narrow path are sunken
into the earth, grass nearly obliterating them.
We start at the beginning, studying the ground

for where to turn in, turn out, go straight.
The nearer the middle, the more defined the curves
and switchbacks, as if those plodding or dancing
ahead of us became tired of it early. Now the children

lose interest. One leaves to clop across a footbridge
in search of trolls, the other lays tiny offerings
at the feet of a stone angel standing guard in runic
mystery. The rest of us follow the labyrinth's

back-and-forth, passing each other coming
and going, staying in our self-imposed lanes. It seems
as if something in us needs edges, needs to be
contained and constrained. We hold fast to our

beliefs, our reasons for keeping things out or in.
We're always wanting walls, as if we'd forgotten
about the sufficiency of sunset, how in spite of them
it happens everywhere. As if we'd forgotten how it is

to be next to woods at dusk, everything holding
its breath, the hair on the back of our necks riffling,
the unseen conductor raising an invisible baton,
then the first ragged notes of the night music.

One Thing Always Is More Important than Another
—line from Stephen Dunn's poem "Midwest"

1. A young spider, dainty as a ballerina, lives under
the bathroom heating unit, venturing out in the open
a few inches or so of an evening. I like to think

it's a *she*, a sort of friend to talk to when I'm there.
I ask her what I can do for her, how she can possibly
survive with nothing to eat since the time weeks ago

that I scooped a fly into the web and watched, gleeful,
as she (or perhaps it was her parent) high-stepped
from under the heater to get a good look at the windfall,

waiting discreetly for it to cease struggling and be still.
One night last week she didn't show up and I worried.
The next night she was back and my joy amazed me.

Now it's November and a few days have passed since
I've seen her. I'm surprised at how much I miss her,
with dinner still to be made, and after that, clean-up.

2. The older granddaughter has taken up the violin. She
mails us tickets for a Facetime concert. We sit in a row
on the couch, in front of the computer. She plucks out
"Mary Had a Little Lamb" and "Old MacDonald."
She says this is called *pizzicato*. She shows us how
bowing works on the open strings. Finally she
smiles her dazzling 11-year-old smile. We applaud
enthusiastically from our living room. Then her sister
picks out "Twinkle Twinkle Little Star" on the piano
with one finger. We clap. She curtsies. They chirp "I love
you!" and blow us many kisses. We blow them back.
We wave goodbye at the screen. This has made our day.

3. The neighbor with the Trump sign in the back of his car stops to chat. I
want to ask what he likes about Trump but don't know how, so instead I ask
about his T-shirt, which says "VETS HOPE". He says he meets once a week
at a church with other vets, some with PTSD. They read the Bible, share
food, listen to each other's stories. I say "That sounds like a really good
thing to be doing," and mean it. He says, "Nice talking to you, love,"
        before we go our separate ways.

How a Poem Happens

Sometimes it appears fully formed,
Athena sprung from Zeus' forehead,
each word named and ordered,
slashes already in place where lines break,
taxing me only to keep it intact
and get it down before it's gone.

Or one will burst in looking for food,
lurch around and help itself to cookies
and when it finally gets down to business,
wear me out with its habit of flinging
words helter-skelter, never finishing
and leaving me to clean up the mess.

I might invite one in, pretty sure it will
remove its shoes at the door and do
without a fuss the grueling work
of stuffing words between the rhymes—
a blind obedience to the poetic foot
reward enough for the numbing task.

Once—it was June, my turn to drive, sun
setting behind as we wound around Ensign Pond,
car windows open to the soft air and the family
sprawled in sleep—one appeared in the mirror
in a sudden blinding flash of golden light
converging with such spring peeper cacophony

that I was left dumb and breathless, gasps
of laughter bubbling up at the secret message
revealed to me: I would be here always, forever
among these teeming ponds, these beeches
tinged pink, on this lovely earth for all time—
and no one awake to contest it.

The only thing I could do then was hold
hard to the wheel, stifle my laughter,
promise to write it all down.

May 11, 1987
   —*for Carol*

Finished up the chemo yesterday.
No more methotrexate drip in veins
short of red and white cells. No more strain
of smiling hard and keeping things at bay
three weeks in a row, head packed in ice to stall
the loss of my hair (because watching my hair
fall out would have just killed me). No more fear.
Won't miss any of it, not at all.

Looking to the future, there's lots of stuff
to do. Here's my list: 1. Remake
my life. 2. Get teeth cleaned (put on hold
for infection risk). 3. Trade in old
Geo for Miata. 4. Summer break—
stock up! 5. Life is funny—laugh!

too many poems about death

in this poem the man
at the KwikStop
SelfServ where I save
5c a gallon because
it's Wednesday is
young & tall &
happy to see me
I can tell by the way
he lopes to the counter
from his task stocking
the back cooler feels like
getting something for
nothing so I buy
TicTacs with my
windfall because he is
leaning chin in hands
smiling at me for the
rest of the giddy
livelong day

In the Medical Building

Seeing these two elderly strangers
step out of the down elevator
leaning on each other,
holding each other up,
hearing their soft murmurings:
Maybe this will be a good thing, and
Yes, maybe it will be OK,
as they move slowly toward the door,

you think, blinking,
*They will make it through anything
as long as they can be together,*
you think, *When they die,
they will die together,*
you think how the tilt
of his head, the way
she holds his arm, remind
you of your parents, and
though you want to follow them out,
to watch over them, to look
for signs and clues,

instead
you turn back to the elevator
that has gone on without you.

Sweeping the Sidewalk

This unseasonably warm
October morning, I spot
clods of dirt on the front walk
left over from my husband's
end-of-season weeding.
It takes me a while
to find the broom and then I am

sweeping the sidewalk
like an old-world hausfrau
in faded dress and apron,
black stockings and sturdy shoes,
as if nothing in the world
could be more important.

Sweeping, I begin to get the why
of it, its everyday necessity:
how the brisk strokes—
left, left, right, right—render
the week's unspeakable news
out of sight, out of mind.
Evil skulks off embarrassed
into the grass.   War
sees me coming, lays down
its arms and surrenders.
Here's Cancer, hiding its shame
in a crack; I send it
skittering sidewise
under the rhododendrons.

For the alchemy to work,
things must be done in order:
Begin at the front steps.
Adopt a wide stance
to show you mean business.
Feel the heft of the broom, the flex
of your wrists as you whisk.
Sweep until everything
has been put in its place.

When you are finished,
pick up the cloak of angst
that has fallen from your shoulders
and toss it in the trash.
Stand the broom in the corner
by the door, to remind you
of what you have accomplished,
what must be done again
tomorrow. You will
hardly be able to wait.

To My Cancer

Listen, you, I'll give it to you straight:
you've overstayed your welcome. You can't stick
around anymore, you're not pulling your weight
and you're wrecking the place. I hereby kick
you out. Scrape up all your slimy stuff,
un-glom yourself from my innards and slink
your sleazy bulk off at once! I've had enough
of your disruption; don't make me make a stink—

you make a mess, you haven't paid the rent,
you stress me out. Once you're gone, I'll find my ease
with the way things are, won't need to know the intent
of my Fates. I'll take back my space, seize
and glean my days of everything they have to give.
I'll watch and feel and listen. I'll stay alive.

Infusion Room
    —for the staff and patients at CVHO

Outside it's cold, overcast. The woman in the recliner across from me
is about to show us how to fashion a chemo head covering out of
a cut-in-half tee shirt. She reaches up to unwrap the one she's wearing.

Her name is Laverne and she's okay with her baldness and glad to show off
the colorful headwear she's made out of the flowery tee. Meanwhile
Nurse Sean is hanging a new IV bag on someone's pole down the aisle

to my left. Laverne stretches the knit fabric across her forehead, smooths
it over her ears, twists it in back with both hands and brings it forward
as an elegant rope holding everything in place. Nurse Tanya comes by

to see if I'm tolerating the taxol without wooziness. *Ta-da!* says Laverne,
ending with a flourish, and the attractive result elicits approving mur-murs
from all the women in the room—the one whose friend has driven her

up from Middlebury at the crack of dawn, the one perched on a folding
chair next to her hooked-up husband, the one sitting upright cross-legged
whose high-school quarterback son is recorded live on her iPhone

pink-haired in honor of his mother. Their drivers, the nurses, me. Even
the usually preoccupied male patients lean forward slightly to watch,
smiling in spite of themselves not to have missed this small miracle.

ode to my bald head

you are still my
base of operations
observations
obsessions
(you think chocolate
milkshake & I
say by all means)

still my fount of ideas
good & bad &
ooh what have we here?
as when together
we came up with
social justice
world peace

you run everything
past my heart
for approval
& my heart is grateful

you convince
my cold feet
it'll all work out
& they warm up

keep mostly straight
what in my quotidian life
is important & what
only niggling
aggravation
(the sun just now
ducking behind a cloud)

think up words
that sound sort of like
poetry

to you I say
thanks so much
& please
grow me some hair

Knotweed

There is no giving up in knotweed,
no thrift in the work of pulling it out
over and over again where it comes back
year after year. The winner of this war
will reclaim a bit of woods for their prize.

I lay siege on it in late summer, after
black fly season, after it's had its own
sweet time to send an army of rhizomes
tunneling underground from the one plant
missed last year behind the cabin

fifty feet into the woods, where it pops up
over there, and over there, upright and brazen
in a ray of sunlight sinking thinly through
the canopy. It's sly enough to avoid
the older, taller trees' deep shade,

and it's relentless. But so am I, clambering
over glacier-tumbled stones, slip-sliding
down the bank into the woods to hunt for
the heart-shaped leaves and jointed stems
taunting me. I will not be outsmarted.

I seek and destroy, seek and destroy,
clutching the noxious plants in one arm,
clawing with my free hand, then staggering
with my haul up the bank and back across
the boulders to the flat grass of the yard.

Today I heard about a museum exhibit
in which the stalks are suspended like wind
chimes. As visitors bump their way through,
the clinking notes produced mix with drone
sounds, creating a thing of beauty. Maybe,

but I prefer vengeance: sweet days of
watching the vile stuff shrivel in slow death.
Sweating, I scatter the stalks over the lawn
to dry, loving the extravagant, meticulous,
gleeful serial killer I have become.

Kindness
 —*for the staff and patients at CVHO*

Our frail neighbor in the Infusion Room
folds her arms across her chest, dwarfing her
even more in the oversized recliner. Nurse
Marie bustles by, says, "Evelyn, why are you
sitting like that? You look like Sitting Bull!"
Evelyn says she's trying to keep warm,
and Marie says, "I can get you a blanket,
would you like a blanket?" Evelyn says
no thanks, she doesn't need a blanket. "Well,"
says Marie, "I'm going to get you one anyway!"
and in a moment she's back with a blanket,
a double-layered white cotton one, heated,
which she tucks carefully around Evelyn, under
her chin, along the sides of her body, beneath
her feet. The IV lines snake out from its edge.
"Now you look like a mummy!" says Marie,
and Evelyn beams up at her, beams at all of us
who have left off our crosswords and naps
to allow this kindness to settle over us,
gather itself around us, some of us even
imagining it seeping into our veins.

Washing Hands during the Pandemic

I'm washing my hands again. It feels like forever:
20 seconds, fingers, thumbs, nails. The water
must be warm. Then dry, preferably with paper
towels, alligator-skin dry. Healing
will have to wait 'til tonight while I'm dreaming
strange dreams. The radio's going, spinning

the latest Coronavirus news, spinning
fake news and truth back to back. In forever-
time at home, I have the freedom to daydream
about a woman president, poetry, clean water
for all. Others do the dirty work, the healing
work, while I worry about toilet paper.

COVID-19 is always the headline. The paper's
heartwarming, terrible news makes my head spin.
Nightly banging on pots may help with the healing,
makes me wonder if we can heal. Yet forever
Navajo people have done without running water—
a mere seven gallons for everything. Dreaming

of clean hands? How many gallons to dream
of a decent life? And the stories in the paper
are mostly about people with plenty of water,
less about people with less, the ones spinning
their wheels on the phone waiting for help forever,
their children hungry. Where is their healing?

Now I hear the governor say the healing's
at hand, there's a sliver of light. He's not just dreaming,
we've flattened the curve, maybe forever,
we've yet to see. Or could this thing be a paper
tiger, meant to scare us? Our planet is spinning
still, struggling to save herself and the water

that gives us life. Washing my hands, watering
my dried-out heart with hope: this is my healing.
My daughter wisely calms herself by spinning
nickels, tweaking them into pirouettes, dreamily.
She's finished the jigsaw puzzle, read the newspaper's
obits and comics. She holds onto forever.

In dreams my hands are cupped to hold water,
the earth forever saved. The morning paper
spins toward the door with news of healing.

Daughter, Spinning
   —*for Jen*

In this time of pandemic,
having come to terms for now
with the news that she won't be
going to work, the bowling alley,
nor any of the other interesting
places that were her routine,

instead she spends her days—
between the two required walks
and the call of a 1000-piece
mind-boggling jigsaw puzzle—
standing at the kitchen counter,
where she keeps her nickels,

spinning them with great dexterity
—a science the rest of us never
have been able to master.
And spin them she does, her
thumb and two fingers tweaking
a coin, setting it on its edge

to twirl gracefully for seconds
before it wobbles and falls flat.
Yesterday all day she mourned
the closing of her favorite
take-out place, couldn't stop,
stood there spinning until she

accustomed herself to the loss
and went out to fetch the mail.
This is usually the way it is:
Spinning pulls her through,
keeps her going, heals her, as
nothing I could ever do, will.

Women of a Certain Age
—for all the older women I know

Women of a certain age
come in a variety of colors
dislike being patronized
are not to be taken for granted

haul creaky bodies to exercise class
work on strength and balance
roll out on hard foam cylinders
know their politics and PBS shows

care for others
teach children to read and be kind
mentor youths who are struggling
build houses for people in need of them

continue their psychotherapy practices
serve as pro bono lawyers
stay in hard jobs beyond retirement
keep working in order to live

run for office for the first time or the twentieth
speak up for social justice
know how to work with others
get things done

write fierce and tender poems
share their joys and vicissitudes
document the past for the rest of us
tell the truth but tell it slant

bounce back from adversity
hold onto hope
believe in something
laugh a lot

if you're not in the habit of saying I love you

start small: whisper it to the plant
you happen to be watering
because it's sprouting out of the earth,

sing it to the soapy dishes in the sink
to show your appreciation
for their slippery fragility,

tell the washing machine how much
you adore it for the work it does
so you don't have to (remembering

the wringer on the old tub washer
your grandmother had back when
it took all day to do the laundry).

Try it out on your pet, baby-talking
"I wub you" into its ear as it lies
grooming itself in your lap.

Sneak it into a bear hug on a small
child, who will pay you back
by drawing you a purple unicorn

frolicking among tulips while
butterflies flit and a yellow sun
perches in a cloudless sky.

Expect the teenager you love to roll
her eyes (a learned response) but say it
anyway; it may show up in her diary.

Tell your parents, even if they're
gone. Give it time; they'll respond;
watch and listen for the signs.

Now that it comes naturally, say it
to your spouse, your lover, your faraway
adult child whenever they're near

or on the phone. Say it in letters
and emails and texts. Every time.
Don't forget. It's bad luck to forget.

A Kuder Preference Test taken by **Anne Bakeman** in 8th Grade indicated that she was destined for a career as either a forest ranger or a torch singer. Instead, she ended up enjoying her stints as an educator at the elementary through university levels. While enrolled in creative writing courses at the University of Vermont in her 40's, she fell hopelessly in love with poetry, because it danced into the room and invited her to play with language and form. She found that writing and reading poetry slow her down, awaken her soul, and help her to understand the perspectives of other living things, including the people she shares a home with—a retired engineer husband and an autistic daughter. She describes herself as a wife, mother and mother-in-law, grandmother, sister and sister-in-law, aunt, friend, ally of people with developmental disabilities and the otherwise disenfranchised, and lover of trees. After surviving five years with ovarian cancer, Anne died on May 14, 2022.

www.ingramcontent.com/pod-product-compliance
Lightning Source LLC
Chambersburg PA
CBHW022122090426
42743CB00008B/961